GEOMETRIC THEMES AND VARIATIONS

4,300 Designs and Motifs

Miguel Angel Sánchez Serrano

DOVER PUBLICATIONS, INC.
Mineola, New York

Bibliographical Note

Geometric Themes and Variations: 4,300 Designs and Motifs is a new work, first published by Dover Publications, Inc., in 2008.

DOVER *Pictorial Archive* SERIES

Library of Congress Cataloging-in-Publication Data

Sánchez Serrano, Miguel Angel.
   Geometric themes and variations : 4,300 designs and motifs / Miguel Angel Sánchez Serrano.
      p. cm. — (Dover pictorial archive series)
   ISBN-13: 978-0-486-46275-2
   ISBN-10: 0-486-46275-7
   1. Repetitive patterns (Decorative arts). 2. Decoration and ornament—Themes, motives. I. Title.
NK1570.S26 2008
745.4—dc22

                                                                    2007034714

Manufactured in the United States of America
Dover Publications, Inc., 31 East 2nd Street, Mineola, N.Y. 11501

NOTE

The extraordinary range and diversity of the original designs in this volume make them an indispensable practical resource for artists and craftspeople. This book is composed of 41 three-page sections, each section filled with variations on a single motif. The inspiration for each new three-page section lies in the simple design element that appears at the top left corner of the first page. Over 4,300 striking designs weave infinite variations on such basic geometric shapes as the circle, square, rectangle, and triangle, as well as more complex and inventive forms, producing a rich and varied trove of motifs ideal for a wide range of projects, including wallpaper and textile design, packaging, and computer art. Among the multitude of designs are a broad spectrum of intricate patterns in a variety of shapes, offering sinuous, circular motifs, interlocking abstracts, kaleidoscopic images, patterns resembling optical illusions, and many more. With this versatile collection, artists and craftspeople will find an almost limitless supply of designs for immediate practical use, as well as a permanent reference ideal for suggesting visual ideas and promoting creativity.

4

8

9

16

18

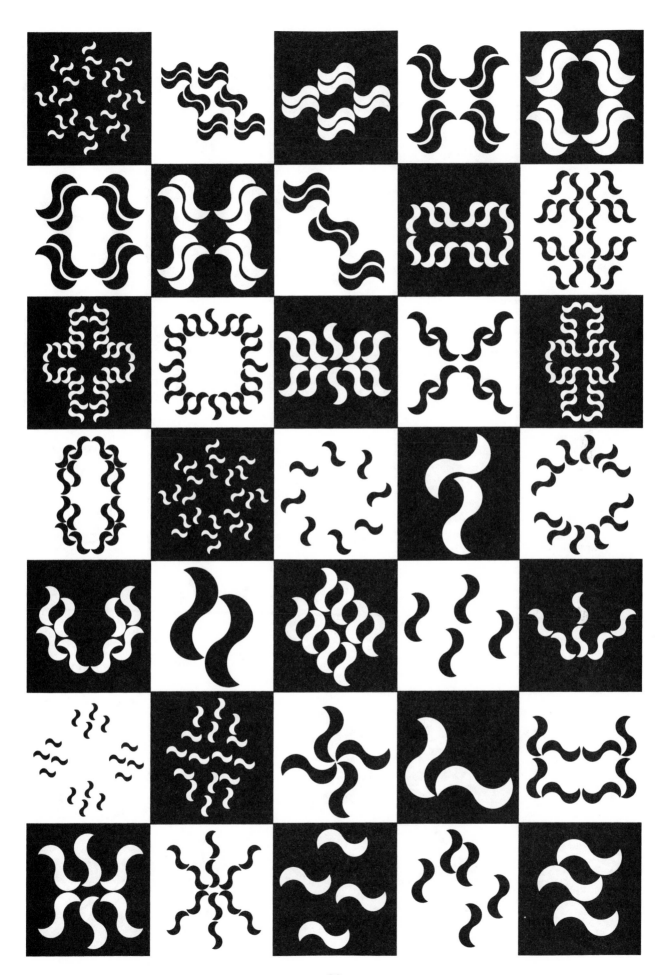

26

31

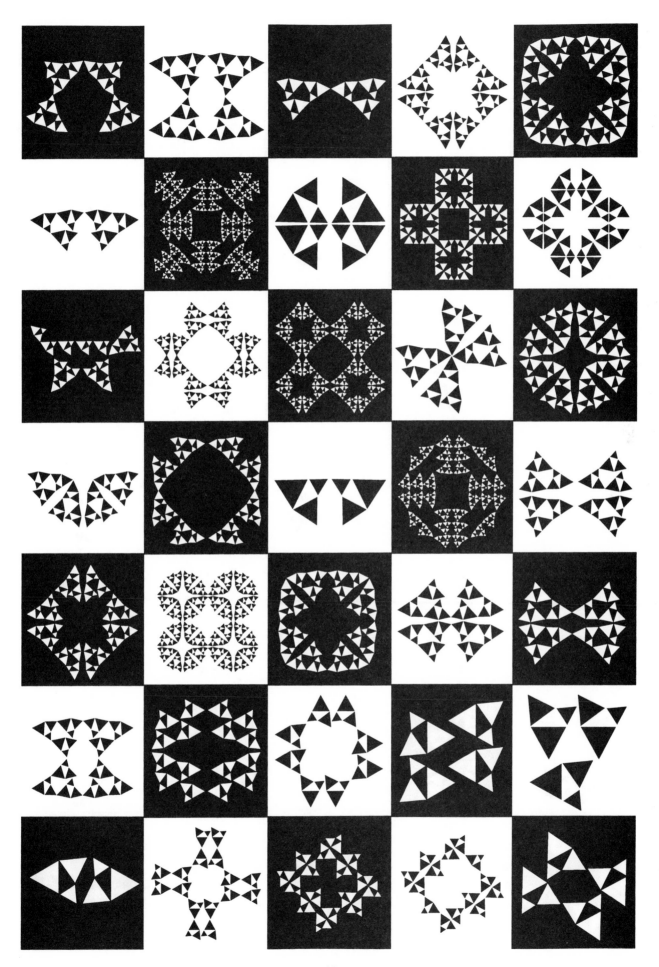

41

42

43

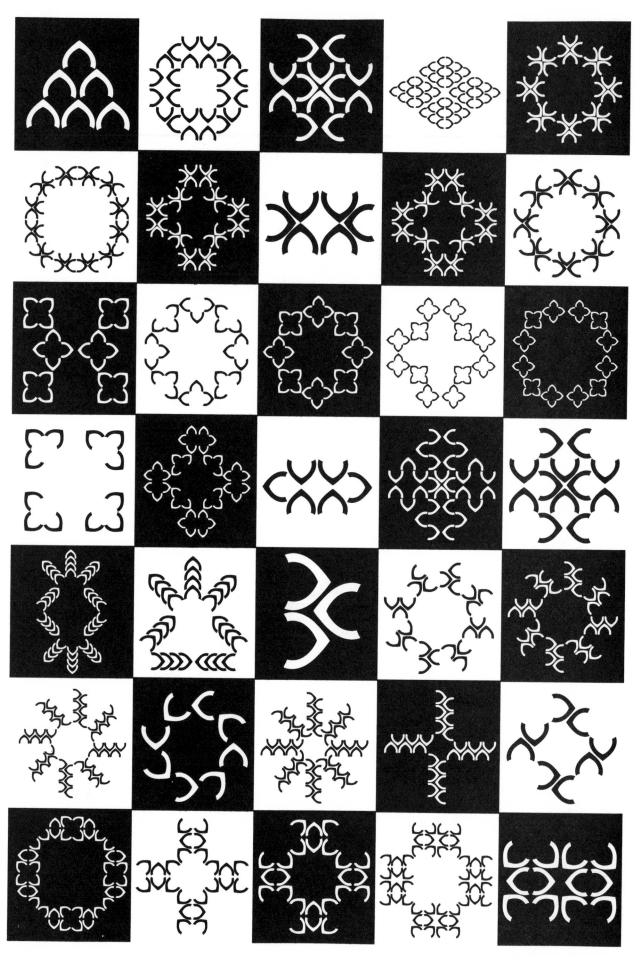

48

49

51

56

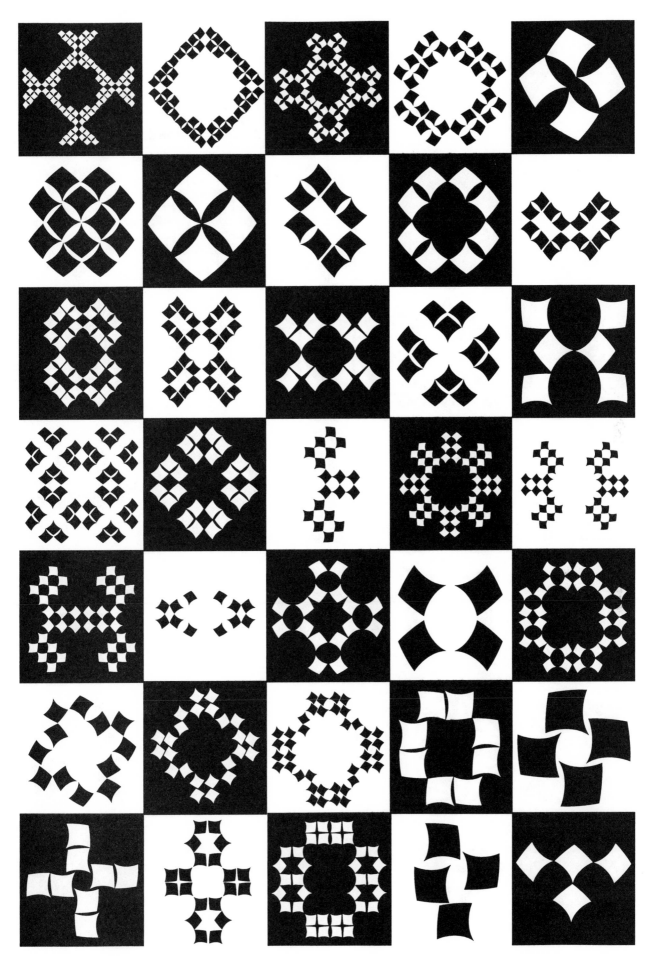

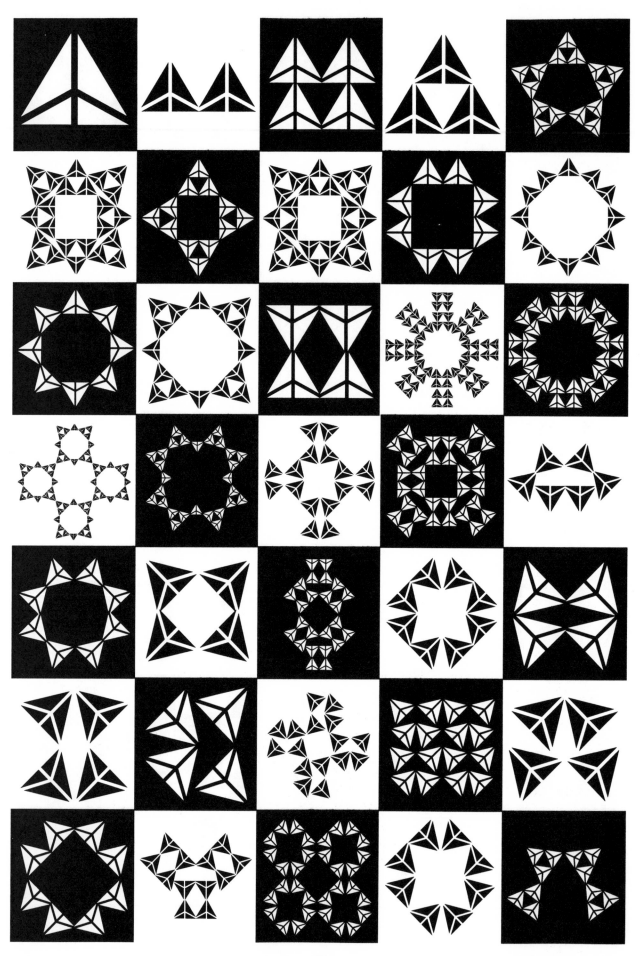

65

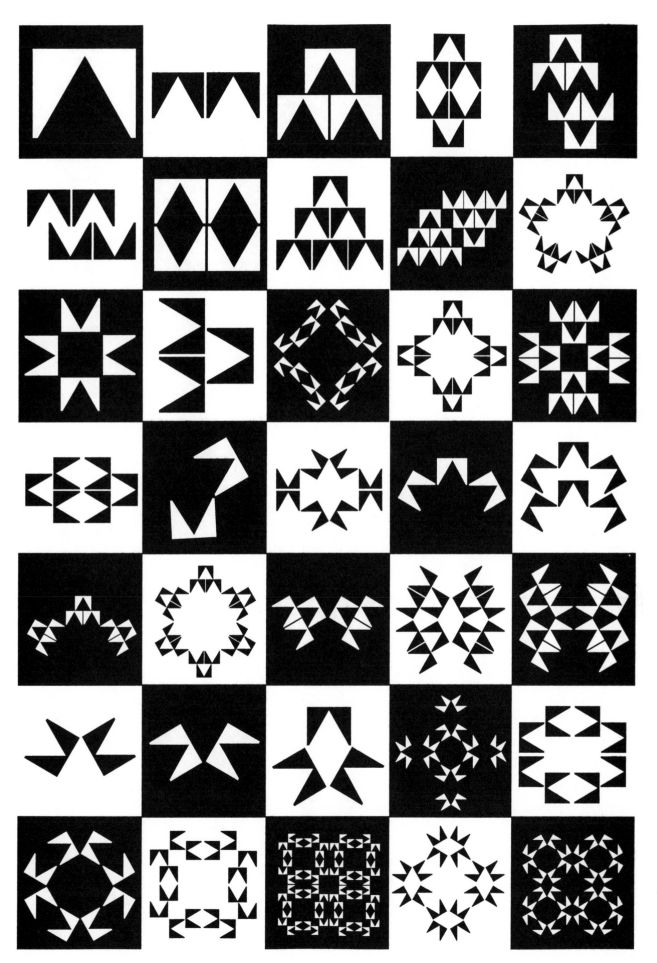

71

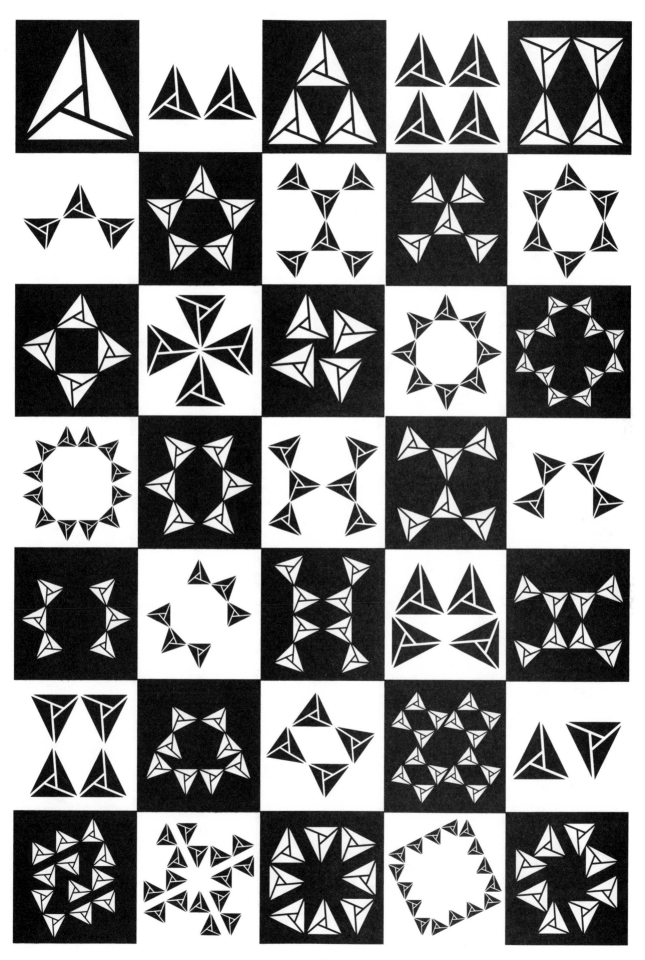

78

84

85

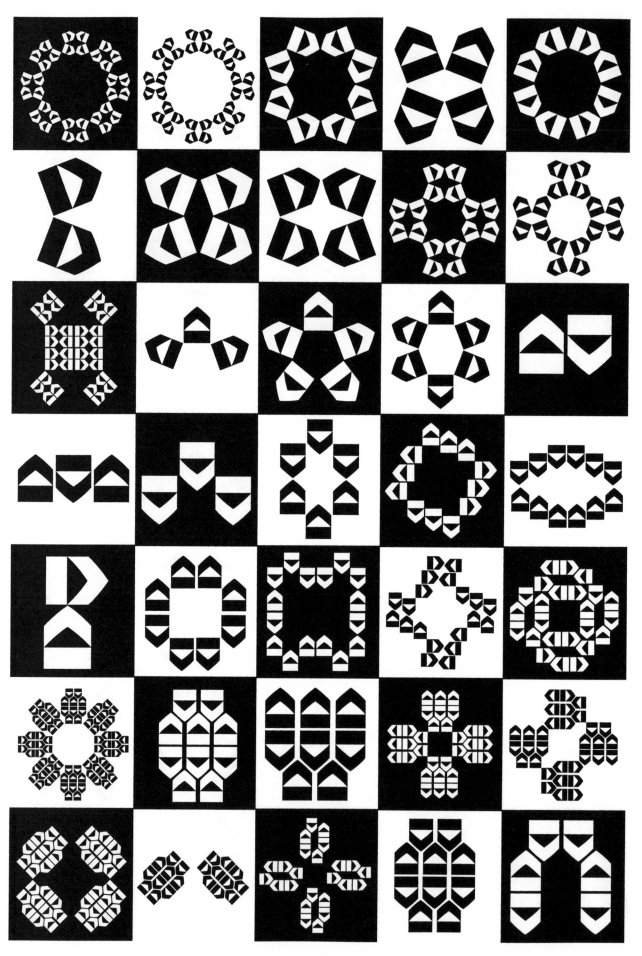

98

99

105

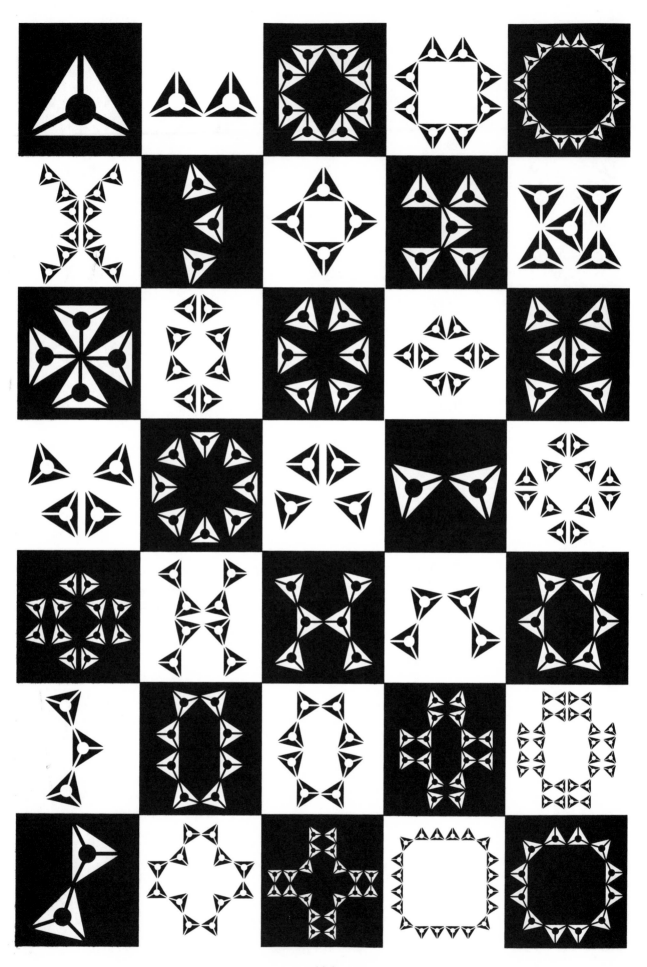

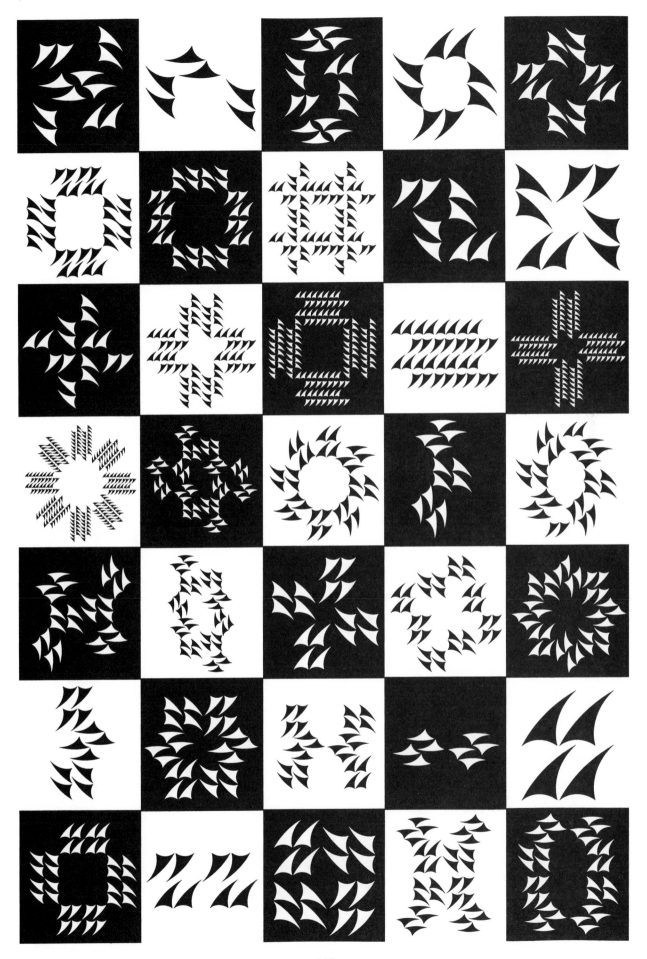

113

114

116